RESTORMEL CA

CORNWALL

Nicholas A D Molyneux

Strategically located above the valley of the river Fowey, and controlling a river crossing, Restormel castle was a powerful symbol of its lord's domination of the surrounding territory.

The castle we see today is a fourteenth-century shell keep (a circular stone wall which enclosed the lord's apartments), with an adjoining bailey or outer court of which little remains. The keep contained prestigious accommodation for the lord and his retinue during their infrequent visits to the castle; the everyday living spaces were in the bailey.

The most prominent owner of the castle was the Black Prince, son of Edward III, who visited the castle twice, once at Christmas 1362. At that time the shell keep was a strident feature in the landscape – its external walls were rendered and limewashed making it appear bright white – and it was surrounded by a deer park. It was a major centre of the Duchy of Cornwall's estates in the fourteenth and fifteenth centuries, and remains part of their estate today.

By the sixteenth century the castle was in poor repair and, apart from a brief flurry of activity during the Civil War, its history is one of neglect and ruin. In the eighteenth century the tenant of the adjoining house took an interest in the site, incorporating it as a picturesque element in his romantic landscape garden.

View from the entrance framed by picturesque planting

CONTENTS

Restormel Castle, detail of print published in 1784

© ROYAL INSTITUTION OF CORNWALL LALr038

Published by English Heritage
1 Waterhouse Square 138 - 142 Holborn
London EC1N 2ST
© English Heritage 2003
First published by English Heritage 2003.
Reprinted 2006, 2008, 2010
Photography by the English Heritage Photographic Unit
and copyright English Heritage unless otherwise stated

Edited by Susannah Charlton
Designed by Pauline Hull
Plan by Richard Morris
Printed in England by Park Communications Ltd
C50 06/10 03578 ISBN 978 1 85074 789 5
Visit our website at www.english-heritage.org.uk

50% recycled
When you have finished with
this leaflet please recycle it

TOUR OF
THE CASTLE

THE BAILEY

Your tour begins outside the ticket office.

You are standing in the bailey or base court of the castle; here, in the fourteenth century, you would have been in the midst of the daily activity connected with the running of a major estate. The stone keep before you has changed little since then, but the bailey was filled with buildings that have now vanished. In 1337 these included a great hall with two cellars (probably above ground), a small chapel, a separate kitchen linked by a covered corridor, three chambers with cellars below and a bakehouse. There was also a gatehouse and stabling for twenty horses.

The much-eroded earth bank and ditch of the bailey lies just behind the ticket office. The far end of the bailey was roughly where you came in at the second gate, and the third side is hidden in the trees. The original entrance lay between the ticket office and the large ditch of the keep on the side nearest the approach road from the valley.

The trees were planted in the late eighteenth century, when the castle was incorporated into a picturesque landscape for the enjoyment of the occupants of Restormel Manor (not open to the public), to the south-east of the castle (see page 22).

THE KEEP

The keep does not stand on the motte, or artificial mound, typical of Norman castles, but rather sits on a natural high point in the middle of a ringwork, or circular ditch and bank. In the late eleventh century there was a bank with a slight stone fortification (timber was difficult to obtain), as well as the ditch enclosing the inner part of the castle. The bank was partly dug away during the building of the substantial circular wall of the keep in the late 13th century.

The ditch and bank that surround the keep

Putlog hole

Now turn right and walk around the outside of the stone keep

From here you get a good impression of the defences: note how the castle sits so prominently in the landscape dominating the river valley. When first built the keep would have been even more pronounced since it would have been plastered on the outside and then limewashed: imagine a white building in the landscape. In the Middle Ages stonework was rarely left unplastered, unless it was of finely cut, ashlar blocks.

There are many small square holes in the walls, known as putlog holes. These are where the builders inserted timber scaffolding poles as they built up the walls. When they had finished they simply sawed off the poles leaving the ends in the wall. As the timber decayed a hole developed, which would have been covered up by the external render. You can see in places that they run in a spiral pattern up the walls.

Notice the large size of most of the windows, and the virtual absence of small openings resembling arrow slits.

SPEARHEAD PHOTOGRAPHY

By the time this wall was built in the fourteenth century the castle was more a status symbol than a serious defensive structure.

On the rear (north-east) side you will find the chapel projecting beyond the main line of the wall (see inside front cover). There is also evidence here for an external timber structure, which is represented by the long horizontal slot in the wall.

THE GATEHOUSE

Having completed the circuit of the outside of the castle you arrive back at the bridge to the gatehouse.

There was once a timber drawbridge that would have been raised to close this outer opening. If you look carefully you can see that the stonework of the bridge is not jointed to the lower part of the gatehouse, which shows that it was built at a different time. As you walk across the bridge, you can see the gap where the two-storey drawbridge tower had a simple timber beam over the external entrance. Behind it lay the gatehouse tower, now largely collapsed, which rose to three storeys. You will see that where it has fallen down it has left a very 'clean' end to the curtain wall on each side, suggesting that the gatehouse was built first to protect the weakest point of the defences, and the curtain wall added later.

Now enter the castle through the inner stone arch.

This arch is one of the best preserved architectural features of the castle. The white stone probably came from Pentewan, 10 miles (16km) to the south-west. It is of high quality and could be carved, unlike the local stone, known as shillet, that was used to build the rest of the castle. As you walk around you will see many ragged edges to openings, where the finest pieces of stone have been stolen.

THE COURTYARD

The space you have entered was the privileged inner sanctum of the castle, and was reserved for the lord and his retinue. Imagine the bustling scene at Christmas 1362, when the Black Prince arrived on horseback with his retinue of attendant knights and ladies, with all their baggage and servants. The large chests full of rich soft furnishings had come on carts in advance, so the castle was already comfortable, the fires lit, and the wine from France ready for drinking. When the lord was not in residence, the business of the castle would have been conducted in the buildings in the bailey. On your left is the Porter's Lodge, under the staircase, from which the porter would have controlled entrance to this part of the castle.

Walk towards the timber staircase on your right. Notice the pit cut into the bedrock at the foot of the staircase, which may be the cellar of a late 11th century tower, filled in late in the 13th century, or a storage pit for food or water.

THE KITCHEN AND SERVERY

The tour of the rooms proceeds anti-clockwise around the courtyard. Enter the kitchen by the first door.

Ahead of you is the main fireplace, which has lost its hood, and the front of the flue. The space above your head would have soared all the way up to the roof, above the tops of the

The inner arch in fine white Pentewan stone

The Black Prince paying homage to his father Edward III

A reconstructed view of the hall in the fourteenth century, showing the storage beneath, and the impressive timber roof.
Compare the drawing of the fireplace with the remains of the original, shown opposite

T BALL

surviving walls, with only limited light from the small windows and the fire.

Here you can see a major feature of the construction of the castle. The inner walls have separated from the circular curtain wall, showing that the curtain wall was built first and the inner walls built up against it. If you look at the putlog holes you will see that they are at different levels on the inside walls from those of the curtain wall, suggesting that the walls are of different dates. But how different? As with all such archaeological dating there is nothing to tell us whether the curtain wall predates the inner walls by one week, or by 100 years. In this case we think that the inner walls were probably built very soon after the curtain wall.

In the east wall of the kitchen (to your left) there is a door and a hatch. They open into the next room, the servery. This had a further door beyond, with another hatchway (rebuilt as a window) looking out into the central courtyard of the castle. The kitchen staff would have passed the food through this hatch to servants who would carry it up an outdoor timber staircase to the hall. The staircase was roofed, ensuring that the food would not have cooled down too much by the time it got to the table. The kitchen staff came under the control of the steward, who was responsible for the feeding of the whole establishment, whilst the personal care of the lord was the province of the chamberlain.

THE HALL CELLAR

As you step into the next room you will discover that it is very large, with two big windows which lit the first-floor room above. You are standing in the cellar and the room above you was the hall, the hub of castle life when the Lord was in residence. He and his household would have dined here every day at trestle tables, and it was where all the feasting and festivities took place. The impressive timber roof structure, befitting its status as the centre of castle life, was supported on stone brackets in the wall between the windows and the fireplace; these have been removed leaving empty slots. The hall was reached by a timber staircase from the central courtyard. The hall cellar was used for storage, and had a heavily beamed ceiling; you can see the large holes in the outside wall for the beams.

CELLAR OF THE LORD'S CHAMBER OR SOLAR

Walk into the next space and look up at the first floor.

This was the lord's chamber or solar, as the private chamber at the head of a medieval hall was called. Like the hall, it had an impressive roof

Remains of the hall fireplace

Solar window. The gate on the right leads to the staircase up to the wall walk

and a fireplace at the far (north) end. At the opposite (south) end there is a recess in the wall, perhaps for a wooden livery cupboard to store provisions to save trips to the kitchen. This was a high-status room, effectively the private quarters of the lord and his family: here he could retire from the hubbub of the hall and have a degree of privacy. It would have contained the best furnishings when he was in residence, particularly the bed which was used to display the grandest fabrics. There was direct access to the wall-walk via a staircase starting at the side of the window. The lord could use this to patrol his walls at leisure, or to receive private visitors.

The east window of the chapel which was blocked during the Civil War for use as a gun platform

THE WELL

Go back into the central courtyard past the well.

The well was dug around 1100 at the time of the first castle. Later, a separate water supply was brought by lead pipe from a spring outside the castle. We do not know the function of the short tunnel, which you can just see leading off the well.

THE CHAPEL

Go into the next room and turn right up the timber staircase to the chapel.

The original access to the chapel was from the lord's chamber or by another external timber staircase rising from the courtyard. Religion played an important part in daily life, and a private chapel was a common feature of large medieval households. This chapel was probably served by the priest from the nearby hermitage (see page 12). If you look back at the arch you can see a few of the original Pentewan stone moulded blocks at each end, although most of the decorative stones have been removed. The main feature, the east window, was blocked during the Civil War in the seventeenth century. You will notice that there are many slots in this wall: during the Civil War these contained supports for a high-level timber platform for cannon (see page

21). In the far right corner there is a piscina, or small arched recess with a drain, for washing the holy vessels.

There may have been a vault beneath, as there is a record in 1783 of the discovery of two skeletons apparently 'locked in each other's arms'. William Masterman, the tenant of Restormel Manor at the time, ordered that the vault be boarded over and filled with earth. No trace of it has been seen in modern times.

THE GUARD ROOM

Returning to the courtyard, turn right and enter the room beside the stone staircase at the end.

Here you can see one of the castle's garderobes (lavatories) in the far right-hand corner. The room seems to have been divided into two by a timber partition (there are two doors into the courtyard), and was for the accommodation of servants or guards. The room above was probably a guest chamber.

THE WALL-WALK

Return to the courtyard and go up the uneven stone staircase on the right of the gatehouse to the wall-walk. Take care on the staircase, which can be slippery when wet.

From here there is a good view of the interior of the keep, and you can also see how effectively the castle commanded the valley.

The tops of the walls were protected by timber hoardings or bratticing. This was a timber structure that hung out over the wall, affording greater protection to defenders, and allowing them to fire downwards on attackers who were close up against

View of the courtyard from the wall-walk

the wall of the castle. It could be dismantled when not needed.

The first room below you was the guest chamber, which would have been occupied by the grander members of the lord's entourage. It has two windows with window seats overlooking the courtyard. This room was accessible only from the courtyard via the stone staircase you have just climbed.

The next room may have been the lady's chamber, a companion to the lord's chamber on the other side of the chapel. She would have accompanied the lord on his progresses, and would have had a suite of furnishings of similar grandeur, including a bed. The lady and her servants reached this chamber either from the courtyard by an external staircase, or from the hall by way of the solar and ante-chapel.

The next room was the ante-chapel, essentially a circulation space, and then the lord's chamber (solar) and hall. Lastly, there was the upper part of the kitchen, which was open to the roof to absorb the smoke and heat from cooking.

Now descend the timber staircase to the courtyard.

Aerial view of the castle in winter, from the south east

© SONIA HALLIDAY PHOTOGRAPHS

A HISTORY OF RESTORMEL CASTLE

ORIGINS

The earliest recorded history of the site is the name itself. Restormel derives from the Celtic words *ros*, meaning a hill spur, and *tor moyl* meaning a bare hill.

The early part of the castle's life is shrouded in mystery but it is more than likely that the castle was one of the many built as a part of the new regime enforced in England following the success of William the Conqueror at the Battle of Hastings in 1066. William was crowned on Christmas Day 1066, but his conquest was only complete in the south east of England. The powerful Godwin family retreated to Exeter, and it was there, early in 1068, that William defeated the local resistance after an eighteen day siege, during which he put out the eyes of a hostage before the walls of the town. There was another rising

in the following year when the men of Devon and Cornwall attacked Exeter, but it was defended by William's lieutenants, whilst he was in the north of England suppressing a much more powerful rebellion.

At the time the Domesday Book was compiled in 1086, Turstin the Sheriff held the manor in which Restormel Castle is located, but there is no mention of the castle. It may

William the Conqueror hunting

The fourteenth-century bridge crossing the River Fowey. Note the way the river has silted up, a process that started soon after it was built

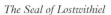

The Seal of Lostwithiel

have been Turstin or his son Baldwin who built the first castle on the site after 1086 in the service of William the Conqueror. One of its chief functions was to defend this crossing of the river Fowey.

A later twelfth-century charter mentions a chapel beside Baldwin's Bridge. This was probably the Hermitage of the Holy Trinity, which lay at the foot of the castle hill on the site of the present-day Restormel Manor.

The earliest castle consisted of an earthwork about 38m (125ft) in diameter with a roughly rectangular bailey. The form of the buildings is not known though the three enigmatic pits dug into the bedrock inside the keep could have been cellars under towers. A fourth pit contains the castle's well, essential if the castle came under sustained attack. The well-chosen site meant that a large mound or motte was unnecessary.

At this time Henry II (1154–89) systematically strengthened the role of central government. This included establishing the system of assizes (the circulating judges) in a south western circuit covering Dorset, Wiltshire, Somerset, Devon and Cornwall. Restormel was in the manor of Bodardle, which in 1166 was held by Robert fitz William, Lord of Cardinham, as the guardian of his wife's brother Walter Hay. When Walter died childless, Robert inherited the estate, and by 1193 it had passed to his grandson Robert of Cardinham, who became one of the King's Justices and was important in the early development of Lostwithiel. Between 1224 and 1227 the estates passed to Robert's son Andrew, and then his daughter Isolda, who married Thomas de Tracy. The end of ownership by local families was a consequence of the rebellion of Simon de Montfort, the Earl of Leceister, against Henry III. A month before de Montfort's defeat at the Battle of Evesham in August 1265, Thomas de Tracy surrendered the castle to Simon de Montfort 'in order that I may avoid the danger and damages of my enemies, who wished to enter that castle, to destroy my barony'. It was during this rebellion that de Montfort summoned a more representative parliament of barons, and it is from this that the idea of the modern English parliament derives.

RICHARD, EARL OF CORNWALL

In 1268 after the restoration of the kingdom to normality, Thomas de Tracy's widow Isolda granted the castle to her feudal overlord Richard, Earl of Cornwall, the younger brother of Henry III. In 1257 Richard had been crowned as monarch designate of the Holy Roman Empire (the successor to the Western Roman Empire, centred in Germany), but he never wielded the power of the office due to his weak character. He was succeeded as Earl of Cornwall by his son Edmund.

Edmund moved some of the administrative functions of Cornwall from Launceston, the eastern gateway to Cornwall, to Lostwithiel. This brought them closer to the areas

This detail of a map of Cornwall, drawn in 1540 by John Leland, shows the extensive deer park around the castle. To the south, note Lostwithiel with its church and bridge, and the much smaller park around Boconnoc House across the river

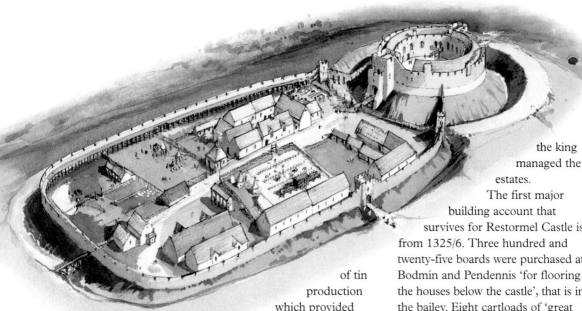

A reconstruction of the castle in the fourteenth century showing the range of timber buildings in the bailey and the stone keep surrounded by its moat

of tin production which provided much of his income. He built the complex of administrative buildings known as the 'Duchy Palace' in Lostwithiel (see page 19) and lived at Restormel Castle. It seems likely that Edmund built the castle in its present form. The evidence suggests it was intended as a symbol of power and status, as it contains no defensive works of any kind, save for the crenellated parapet. Instead of arrow slits there are large windows for the principal rooms and small ones lighting the staircases and lavatories. It is likely that the castle functioned chiefly as a lordly residence and estate, and for hunting.

Edmund died without heirs in 1299 and the title of Earl of Cornwall reverted to the Crown, meaning that the king managed the estates.

The first major building account that survives for Restormel Castle is from 1325/6. Three hundred and twenty-five boards were purchased at Bodmin and Pendennis 'for flooring the houses below the castle', that is in the bailey. Eight cartloads of 'great timber' came from Penlyn and 45kg (100lb) of lead for roofing the houses. Initially the lead was carried from the castle into the town for weighing at the scales in the Duchy Palace to avoid fraud, but this was evidently too cumbersome and 'the lord king's scale [was moved] from Lostwithiel to Restormel'. Thousands of stone slates for roofing came by boat from Golant and Fowey, and laths from the Earl's own woods in the park of Penlyn, from Liskirret Park and Fowey. But the biggest item recorded in the accounts is the £9 10s (£9.50p) paid to the two men roofing 'the great hall and certain chambers outside the castle', at a time when a craftsman was paid about four old pence (2p) a week.

TIN-WORKING AND THE
❖ STANNARIES ❖

In the Middle Ages the tin industry in Cornwall and Devon was of great economic importance. Tin ore occurs extensively in Cornwall, and in this period it was not mined but 'streamed' from alluvial deposits close to streams and rivers. The water was used to wash away the lighter minerals, then the ore was smelted in small stone buildings known as 'blowing houses'. The tin was then 'coined', a process which entailed weighing, assaying (testing for quality) and stamping. Finally it was sold to merchants, usually for export.

In the twelfth century a special legal and taxation system began to evolve to enable the Crown to manage and control the tin industry. The system was administered through eight Stannaries or districts (the word 'stannary' derives from the Latin *stanum* meaning tin). The four Stannaries in Cornwall came together under a Convocation or Parliament empowered to make laws relating to the tin industry and those involved in it, including workers, owners and merchants. In return for heavy taxation on tin, they were exempt from most other taxes, among other privileges.

The Cornish Convocation was based in Lostwithiel, and in the 1290s the Earl of Cornwall created the Duchy Palace as their headquarters. It included a prison, warehouse and space for the Convocation meetings. A fragment of the original buildings still stands in the centre of Lostwithiel, giving some idea of the scale and quality of the whole complex.

Lostwithiel itself was a new town created by the Earls of Cornwall in the twelfth century and probably owes its origins to the tin industry. The core of the historic town is carefully planned on a small-scale grid system, indicating that it was a deliberately created settlement at the lowest crossing point of the river Fowey.

By the fourteenth century there was concern that the prosperity of the town was threatened by the silting of the harbour. This, ironically, was a direct result of the tin streaming which was sending silt and sand down the river. However, these fears were not realised until many centuries later, and indeed barges were still able to reach the town for trade in the nineteenth century.

BRITISH LIBRARY/BOOK OF 1561 DE RE METALLICA

Sixteenth-century woodcut showing tin-streaming, as it would have been done in Cornwall

THE FIRST DUKE OF CORNWALL

In 1337 Edward of Woodstock or 'the Black Prince', eldest son of Edward III, was given the newly created title Duke of Cornwall. The estates attached to this title included 'the castle and manor of Restormel with the park in the same county ... and the town of Lostwithiel'. A major survey of the estate that year included the first detailed description of Restormel Castle:

There is there a castle well walled. And there are within the walls of the said castle, a hall, three chambers and as many cellars. One chapel where the glass of the larger windows is broken for the most part and needs speedy repair if it is not to become worse. (One stone image of blessed Mary in the same chapel, valuable, as it is said, being of alabaster.)... And there are beyond the gate of the said castle a great hall with two cellars and a sufficient chapel...And there is there a certain conduit of water made of lead through which water is brought into the castle to each house of office of the same castle which needs new repair with lead.

This is the first reference to one of the signs of luxury in the castle, the provision of a piped water supply. It shows that there were two sets of apartments, one in the keep for the use of Edmund, Earl of Cornwall, and another in the bailey. The bailey was used for the day-to-day running

Reconstruction of the castle courtyard in the fourteenth century showing the roofed stairway up to the hall on the left

T BALL

of the estate, while the buildings within the keep were reserved for the lord. In the bailey there was a great hall with a detached kitchen linked by a corridor. Most of the bailey buildings were built of stone with timber roofs. Despite the works recorded only a few years previously, the castle appears to have been in need of repair. It was not unusual to renovate only when the

THE BLACK PRINCE

Edward of Woodstock, as his contemporaries knew him, was born on 15 June 1330 at Woodstock, Oxfordshire, the eldest son of Edward III. His father bestowed many titles on him, in the expectation that he would one day be king. He was created Earl of Chester in 1333, first Duke of Cornwall in 1337, Prince of Wales in 1342 and Prince of Aquitaine in 1362. In 1348 Edward III created a new order of chivalry, the Order of the Garter, intended to be a recreation of King Arthur's knights of the round table. He made his son a founder member of this prestigious order, which survives today.

Edward was undoubtedly a great fighter of considerable chivalry, renowned for his generous treatment of the imprisoned French king after the Black Prince's victory at Poitiers. He was not generally known as the Black Prince until the

The Black Prince's Effigy in Canterbury Cathedral

sixteenth century, although a contemporary French writer described him *'en armure noire en fer bruni'* (in black armour of burnished steel) during his first great victory at Crécy in France (1346), fought when he was only sixteen. The battle was an early success in Edward III's campaign to win the French throne at the start of the Hundred Years War

(which ebbed and flowed across Europe from 1337 until 1453).

In 1361 Prince Edward married Joan, the young widow of Thomas, Earl of Kent. Soon afterwards in 1363 the prince embarked in great style with his entourage to take charge of the English owned territory of Aquitaine, establishing his court at Bordeaux as one of the most glittering in Europe, with the young Prince at the height of his powers.

Sadly Edward's last few years were less than glorious. He suffered defeats on the battlefield and caught an infection while fighting in Spain that slowly debilitated him during the last years of his life. He returned to England in 1371 and died on 8 June 1376 at Westminster, the year before his father, so that his expectation of ascending the throne was never fulfilled. That position went instead to his son, the future Richard II.

A F KERSTING

Early fifteenth-century tournament scene taken from an illuminated manuscript of the legends of King Arthur

owner was about to visit and, of the many buildings, probably only those in daily use were repaired.

At this date the deer park that surrounded the castle contained about 300 deer, for the lord's enjoyment as a huntsman and at his table. The lord was also able to use them as convenient gifts when he wanted to flatter somebody with their importance. Such a herd was considered an essential attribute of the country estate at this period, and this was the largest in Cornwall.

Despite his heavy commitments elsewhere, notably fighting on his father's behalf in France and Spain, the Black Prince found the time to visit Restormel Castle twice in his life. The earliest record of personal interest is recorded in 1351 when he ordered that 'for the safety of his duchy of Cornwall and the people of the country in this time of war', his four castles in Cornwall should be

'speedily repaired'. If it became necessary to garrison the castle he ordered that the feudal estates were to supply men who were to dwell there for forty days supplying their own food.

On 21 May 1354 the first signs of preparations for a visit by the prince to Restormel are found in an order to repair all 'the prince's castles and manors of Cornwall, as well as the conduit within the castle of Restormel'. The prince and his high-ranking guests would have brought their own servants and baggage, so the party would have been at least 40 or 50 people with horses.

The visit itself took place in the late summer of 1354, which was a time of disaster. The first major outbreak of bubonic plague, or 'Black Death', had occurred in 1348–9 and there were at least two further outbreaks in 1361–2 and 1369. During the epidemic half the population of England perished. Simultaneously vast numbers of cattle and sheep died of a 'murrain' or plague. The records of the prince's visit are slender but show that he signed various orders at Restormel Castle from 24 August to 2 September.

Six years after his visit, in 1360, the prince ordered that his castles in Cornwall be made ready for conflict,

❖ THE DUCHY OF CORNWALL ❖

This institution was established in 1337 when the Black Prince was created the first Duke of Cornwall at the age of seven. On receiving the title the prince was given all the estates of the defunct Earldom of Cornwall, including the castles of Launceston, Restormel, Tintagel and Trematon, a fortified manor house at Liskeard, and the 'Duchy Palace' at Lostwithiel. There were many other properties outside Cornwall such as the castles of Berkhamstead (Herts) and Wallingford (Berks).

A permanent staff of officials was created in Cornwall, led by the Receiver, and an advisory council, imitating on a small scale the royal administration. This structure has been followed by subsequent dukes.

From the time of the Black Prince onwards, the title Duke of Cornwall has been automatically bestowed on the eldest son and heir of the reigning monarch from birth. This distinguishes it from the earldom of Chester and the principality of Wales, both also held by the monarch's eldest son, which are conferred by special investiture. When there is no duke the estates revert back to the monarch, although the Duchy administration continues as a separate entity.

Throughout most of the medieval period the castles of the Duchy were kept in reasonable repair. In the 1540s, however, they were effectively replaced by Henry VIII's new coastal castles at St Mawes and Pendennis, and were finally allowed to fall into ruin.

For the fifty-five years after Henry VIII's death there was no duke, and when the title passed to Prince Henry (son of James I) in 1603, the Duchy possessions had been so long 'disgraced by the waste of Princely presence' that their decline was irreversible. Nevertheless, the estates continued to provide a substantial income for the future king. In Cornwall the tax on tin produced significant sums of money.

Of the twenty-four dukes to date only thirteen have lived to become monarchs. The longest-serving duke was the future Edward VII, who held the title from his birth in 1841 until he succeeded his mother, Queen Victoria, in 1901.

HRH Prince Charles inherited the title in 1952 and is the twenty-fourth Duke of Cornwall. He retains substantial lands in Cornwall, although the majority of Duchy land lies outside Cornwall.

Ruins of Lostwithiel Palace as they were in the eighteenth century

CORNISH STUDIES LIBRARY

'not knowing how the future will turn out or what perils may arise during his absence from the realm'.

CHRISTMAS AT RESTORMEL

Christmas 1362 was a high point in the history of the castle. On 11 November notice was issued to the prince's faithful retainer, John de Kendale, constable and receiver of Restormel Castle, that 'the prince intends to come presently to the castle of Restormel, and stay there for Christmas'.

Christmas was a great period of feasting, the centre piece of which was the Yule boar: a real one for the wealthy, a boar-shaped pie for everybody else, accompanied by French wine and English beer. Churches, castles and houses were decorated with ivy, mistletoe, and holly. We can imagine the prince watching the local mummers performing, and enjoying the music of the harp and the lute. The feasting ended on the Feast of the Epiphany, 6 January, and the decorations finally came down on Candlemas Eve, 1 February. The giving of presents was another important part of the celebrations, but they were not given on Christmas Day, but rather on New Year's Day.

The prince's visit took place against the background of his impending departure for France. On 19 July 1362 he had been created Prince of Aquitaine by the King, his most prestigious title, bringing with it large estates in the English-ruled area around Bordeaux. As a consequence, by Christmas he was making preparations to remove his entire household to France in order to rule over his new principality. The final date on which we know the prince was at Restormel was 10 April 1363 when he signed an order before sailing from Plymouth in June.

In the Black Prince's time the castle would usually have been bare save for painted plasterwork. Furniture or soft furnishings normally travelled with noble and royal households, which spent much of their time moving from one house or castle to another. Tapestries were popular as they could be packed away in chests and hung up at the next stop. Some idea of the luxury of the Black Prince's life can be seen in his will, which left his 'great bed' to his son, 'embroidered with angels, with the pillows, carpets, coverlets, sheets and all other apparel belonging to the said bed'.

Along with some other fragments of decorated glass, this exquisite glass beaker was dug up in the moat at Restormel in 1880 by James Runnals, an estate worker. Made in Venice in the fourteenth century, it could well have been used by the Black Prince himself. It is now in the collection of the British Museum

BRITISH MUSEUM

THE CASTLE IN DECLINE

The Black Prince died in 1376. Subsequently there is little sign of much interest being taken in Restormel Castle by the Dukes of Cornwall, though there were sporadic attempts to keep it in repair.

In the lord's absence, the estate was run by the estate officials living and working in the bailey. Troops would only have been garrisoned here in times of uncertainty.

The decay of the castle is first recorded by John Leland in his famous Itinerary, a record of his travels around England in the 1530s. Leland commented that 'The Base Court is sore defacid, [but] the fair large Dungeon [keep] yet stondith'.

THE CIVIL WAR

Restormel Castle saw its only serious military action during the Civil War. A Parliamentary army led by Lord Essex held Lostwithiel and Fowey briefly as it retreated through Cornwall away from the advancing Royalist army in 1644. However, the castle was captured on 21 August 1644 by the Royalist Sir Richard Grenville, Lord Essex was defeated and he eventually fled Cornwall in a small boat from Saltash, briefly giving the Royalists the upper hand. The event was described by a contemporary diarist, a Royalist:

Engraving of the castle by the Bucks dating from 1734

THE WEST VIEW OF RESTORMEL CASTLE, IN THE COUNTY OF CORNWALL.

Lestormel, or Restormel, or as others write, Lestmel Castle, was one of ye most Ancient & principal Seats of the British Dukes of Cornwall & others, long before ye Conquest. The Town of Lestwithiel was anciently on this hill till ye people & their prince for conveniency of ye River Foy, mov'd lower down. The Dukes of Cornwall had a park here till it was dispark'd by KHVIII.

Sir Richard Grenville with 700 men pelted the rogues from their hedges… near Trinity (Restormyn) Castle – which Castle was this morning surprised by Sir Richard Grenville's men, and some thirty of the rebels taken, and divers barrels of beefe.

It was at this time that the east window of the chapel was filled with masonry and a gun platform constructed above the chapel at wall-walk level to improve the castle's defences.

A PICTURESQUE GARDEN

In 1753 the lease of Trinity House and its park was sold to Thomas Jones, a lawyer who retired here from his practice in St Austell. Trinity House (now Restormel Manor) stands at the bottom of the valley on the site of the Hermitage of the Holy Trinity. The lease did not include the castle ruins, which were retained by the Duchy of Cornwall, but this did not deter Jones from spending a good deal of money on them. In the late eighteenth century there was a taste for Picturesque gardens, imitating the paintings of Claude Lorrain or Gaspar Poussin, which featured a 'natural' landscape of hills and trees, contrived to give views of romantic, ivy-clad ruins. Jones seems to have used Restormel Castle to provide a similar prospect from his home.

In 1776 Thomas Jones bequeathed the lease of the house and park to his niece's husband William Masterman, who served as MP for Bodmin from 1780 to 1784. Masterman renamed the house Restormel House and lived there until his death in 1786. It was then let to John Hext, whose family continued in residence until the early years of the twentieth century.

The garden, created by William Masterman in about 1784, was described by Charles Sandoe Gilbert in his Historical Survey of the County of Cornwall in 1820:

The terrace and winding walks … are carried through the plantations that wave over the mount, and shelter this mouldering ruin …. At the foot of the mount, on the eastern side, stands RESTORMEL HOUSE, which is built in the castle style, with its walls embattled, and commanding a perspective view of a delightfully wooded valley…

A ROYAL VISIT

In 1846 the castle received its first royal visit for several hundred years. Queen Victoria was in Cornwall on the Royal yacht, which moored at Fowey, from where she took a carriage to Lostwithiel and Restormel. The queen recorded the visit in her journal as follows:

ROYAL INSTITUTION OF CORNWALL

... surrounded by woods, stands a circular ruin, covered with ivy, of the old castle of Restormel, belonging to the Duchy of Cornwall .... It was very picturesque from this point.

We visited here the Restormel mine, belonging also to the Duchy of Cornwall. ... Albert and I got into one of the trucks and were dragged in by miners .... Albert and the gentlemen wore miners' hats.

In 1865 the castle was visited by Queen Victoria's son, the future Edward VII, who was then Duke of Cornwall (as well as Prince of Wales). The prince, together with Princess Alexandra, arrived at Fowey in their yacht.

In 1925 the Duchy of Cornwall passed the guardianship of the castle to the Ministry of Works. The castle was cleared with typical ministry thoroughness, removing the enveloping, if picturesque, ivy and allowing the stonework of the castle to be conserved. Today the castle is still owned by the Duchy of Cornwall, but it has been looked after by English Heritage, the country's leading conservation body, since its creation in 1984.

Victorians visiting the ruins which were described by F W L Stockdale as 'richly overgrown with ivy, and being almost embosomed in wood, are very pleasing objects to the lovers of the picturesque'. (Excursions in the County of Cornwall, 1824)

FURTHER READING

Barber, Richard, 1978, *Edward, Prince of Wales and Aquitaine: A biography of the Black Prince*, London

Harvey, John, 1976, *The Black Prince and his age*, London

Henderson, C, 1935, *Essays in Cornish History*, Oxford

Hext, F M, 1891, *Memorials of Lostwithiel: Collected and Contributed*, Truro

Hull, P L, (ed) 1971, 'The Caption of Seisin of The Duchy of Cornwall' (1337) *Devon & Cornwall Record Society* **NS 17**

McAleavy, Tony, 1998, *Life in a Medieval Castle*, London

Pennington, Robert R, 1973, *Stannary Laws. A History of the Mining Law of Cornwall and Devon*, Newton Abbot

Lostwithiel from Restormel